THEN & NOW

POTRERO HILL

Opposite: Perhaps the romance between the professional photographer and Potrero Hill began in 1922 when this publicity photograph of a Dart automobile (probably unrelated to the Dodge Dart) was taken. In years since, the hill's dramatic views and wide streets have attracted many print advertisers, filmmakers, and producers of television shows and commercials. The hill has been featured in many filmed car chases, most notably in the 1968 movie *Bullitt*, starring Steve McQueen. In the 1990s, an episode of the television series *Nash Bridges* showed a car hurtling through the windows of the Michael-Gary and Company hair salon on the corner of Twentieth and Arkansas Streets. More recently, Volkswagen photographed one of its latest models parked in front of colorful new condos on De Haro Street. (Courtesy private collector.)

THEN & NOW

POTRERO HILL

Peter Linenthal
Abigail Johnston

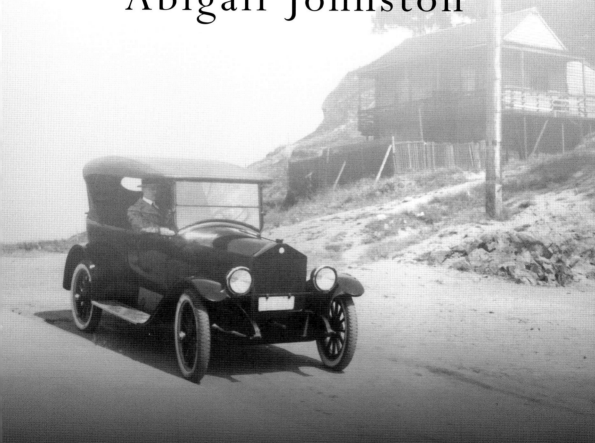

Copyright © 2009 by Peter Linenthal and Abigail Johnston
ISBN 978-0-7385-5966-7

Library of Congress Control Number: 2008928806

Published by Arcadia Publishing
Charleston SC, Chicago IL, Portsmouth NH, San Francisco CA

Printed in the United States of America

For all general information contact Arcadia Publishing at:
Telephone 843-853-2070
Fax 843-853-0044
E-mail sales@arcadiapublishing.com
For customer service and orders:
Toll-Free 1-888-313-2665

Visit us on the Internet at www.arcadiapublishing.com

ON THE FRONT COVER: Behind the house to the left once stood what was probably the first house built on Potrero Hill, an adobe possibly constructed by the De Haro family in the 1840s when they held the grant to the new pasture, Potrero Nuevo, of Mission Dolores. Much has changed since the 1900 image was taken, but the view north from these homes is still amazing, and the hill is just as steep. (Then image, courtesy California Historical Society, FN-22184.)

ON THE BACK COVER: This photograph was taken from the top of Carolina Street looking west along Southern Heights Avenue shortly after it was cut between Carolina and Rhode Island Streets in 1924. To make way for this street, originally called Diagonal Street, the Potrero Hill Neighborhood House was moved 90 feet north of its original location to where it stands today (in the Now photograph on the bottom of p. 33) on the northeast corner of De Haro Street and Southern Heights Avenue.

CONTENTS

ACKNOWLEDGMENTS

We thank everyone who has generously shared photographs, memories, and family stories with the Potrero Hill Archives Project for more than 20 years. Many of their names, stories, and pictures are in the pages that follow. Without them, this book would not have been possible.

We would also like to thank Philip Anasovich, Lew Baer, Julia Bergman, John Borg, Joe Boss, Janet Carpinelli, Florindo Cimino, Sarah Davis, Philip DeAndrade, Babette Drefke, Stephen Fotter, Paul Fromberg of St. Gregory of Nyassa Church, Gregg Gaar, Sina Ghaemmaghami, Frank Gilson, Ed Hamilton, Lia Hillman of the Potrero Branch Library, Pete Hogg and Phil Bond of Digital Pond, Don Kambic, Glenn Koch, Jennifer Lang, Melinda Lee, Mark Linenthal, Judie Lopez, Pete Luskutoff, Dave Margulius, Milton Newman, Kevin O'Connell, Rose Marie Ostler, the Potrero Hill Association of Merchants and Businesses, Saint Teresa's Church, Newall Snyder, Susan Snyder of the Bancroft Library, Martin Spencer-Davies, Luke Stuart of Catellus, Virginia Sustarich, Fran Taylor, Christopher VerPlanck, Peter Walbridge of Big Think Studios, Ralph Wilson, Natalie Wisniewski, and Lester Zeidman. We are deeply grateful to Susan Goldstein and Christina Moretta of the San Francisco History Center at the Main Library, and to Mary Morganti, Debra Kaufman, Philip Adam, and Alison Moore of the California Historical Society. And once again, we thank our patient and understanding editor, John Poultney.

Unless otherwise credited, the Then photographs in this book are courtesy of the Potrero Hill Archives Project, and the Now photographs were taken by Peter Linenthal. The San Francisco History Center of the San Francisco Public Library (SFPL) also provided many of the historic images.

INTRODUCTION

My introduction to San Francisco was the old Third Street train station where I arrived in 1970, somewhat accidentally and close to penniless. I crashed with friends out in the Avenues and found a job at a small drafting equipment supply house on Minnesota and Twenty-sixth Streets. I didn't know where I was going each day—neither did my friends. I just knew what buses would get me there and back. There were no lunch places nearby, so my fellow employees and I depended on the visits of a Roach Coach. Sometimes we would head for hot dogs, beer, and a game of pool at the old Mission Rock Resort. Most of the other customers were local fishermen who rented rowboats there and cleaned their catches on the back deck. After hanging up our cue sticks, we would stop at the Tick-Tock diner (where Carlos Santana once worked as a dishwasher) on Third Street for coffee to get us through the rest of the day.

A year later, at a different job, I met a guy with a ponytail who lived in a cottage on Mariposa Street. Two enduring relationships began in earnest then—one with a person, the other with a place. Thirteen years and two apartments later, we sought our own house on the hill. The prices were outrageous—$189,000 for a small, undistinguished two-family on Connecticut Street! Reluctantly, we looked elsewhere, and in 1986, we moved into a fixer-upper on Florida Street.

I came to know Potrero Hill better after I no longer lived on it. I was volunteering at the *Potrero View* when we moved, pasting up the newspaper's pages with rubber cement in the paper's funky office in the Neighborhood House's kindergarten building on Carolina Street. I kept at it for the next 20 years. Over time, the technology improved somewhat, and there I met Peter Linenthal, who often supplied the paper with treasures from the Potrero Hill Archives Project. Another enduring relationship was born.

—Abigail Johnston

My earliest memories of the hill are warm ones. I was driven across town to kindergarten in the brown-shingled Potrero Hill Neighborhood House. I remember the sweet cubes of harvard beets we ate at lunch and the easels with pots of paint and brushes. Potrero Hill was quieter than the rest of the city, with wide streets open to the sky, sunny and windy. In 1975, I bought a house on Missouri Street and could see the Neighborhood House from my back window. I joined the Potrero Hill Archives Project, first recording oral histories, then collecting anything to do with the hill and holding a "History Night" each October.

This book reminds me that although dramatic change has been a constant on the hill, there are still plenty of spots that *San Francisco Bay Guardian* founder Bruce Brugmann calls "Links to the Past." Some, such as the Neighborhood House, designed by Julia Morgan, are well known. Other places seem like secrets, places you discover. Walk through the gateway to General Hospital's Mental Health Rehabilitation Center on Potrero Avenue, and you will find a small stone grotto. It once ornamented the garden of St. Catherine's Home for wayward girls. Look up at the keystone block of the tunnel at the Twenty-second and Pennsylvania Caltrain Station; it is incised "1905."

Guidebooks once ignored Potrero Hill, but not anymore. We have been discovered. On Halloween, the stream of kids coming to my door gets longer each year, and their homemade costumes are great. Young families are moving to the neighborhood. And although each year there are fewer of the really old-timers, there is a new generation of longtime residents on the way. I am becoming one of them.

—Peter Linenthal

Our first book for Arcadia Publishing, Images of America: *San Francisco's Potrero Hill*, was a chronological history of the neighborhood. We have arranged this book geographically. Potrero Hill has such topographic variety that we constantly discovered new views. We explored photo collections too, and we found images that were surprising, informative, and sometimes beautiful. Seeking "Now" images to pair with wonderful "Thens" has been exhilarating and challenging. Houses, hillsides, and even whole streets are gone or completely transformed. And there are so many more trees now than there were then! We invite visitors and longtime residents to take a walk with us through streets and decades of Potrero Hill, a walk we hope will give a deeper sense of a place we love.

—Peter Linenthal and Abigail Johnston

DESCRIPTIONS OF POTRERO HILL THROUGH THE CENTURIES

The northern tip of the San Francisco Peninsula, which was within Yelamu tribal territory, was the most desolate of the San Francisco Bay Region tribal landscapes. Much of the area was covered with windswept sand dunes and the scrubbiest of grasslands. Its creeks were small and it lacked extensive oak groves. The Yelamus, no more than 160 individuals, spent much of the year split into . . . semi-sedentary village groups. One group moved seasonally along Mission Creek, from Sitlintac on the Bay shore to Chutchui two or three miles further inland.
—*A Time of Little Choice: The Disintegration of Tribal Culture in the San Francisco Bay Area 1769–1810*, Randall Milliken, Ballena Press, 1995

There is no portion of San Francisco where the work of "the mighty hand of man" is shown so plainly, perhaps, as in that district known as the Potrero. . . . The pioneers of progress at the Potrero have had first actually to create the very ground upon which have been erected those vast establishments that have given to the district its name and fame as the very foremost center of mechanical industry and wealth-producing enterprises upon the Coast. . . . Where the massive factories now stand solidly along the level shore, which bristles with its rows of piers, was once but a choice between precipitous hillsides, along which a goat could scarcely make his way, and oozy foul-smelling marshes, a mere glance at which would seem sufficient to have utterly discouraged the most progressive combination of energy and capital.
—"The Potrero as It Is," *San Francisco Examiner*, August 11, 1889

A good many people of this city actually do not know where the Potrero District is. . . . It is built on the southern heights, and is often called so. The northern boundary is Townsend; its eastern side is San Francisco bay; Army Street borders the south, while Potrero Avenue encloses it on the west. . . . Cattle grazing is not carried on as it was when the state was admitted into the union. Only the name Potrero [pasture] still lives to remind us of this bygone occupation.
—From an issue of the *San Francisco Call*, November 23, 1912, written and edited by students at Irving M. Scott School

Last March, when 752 Carolina Street came on the market as the highest-priced home ever to sell in Potrero Hill, people thought who is going to spend $3 million in Potrero Hill? Nine days later, the home sold for at least the sticker price (the final sales price was never disclosed).
—From the blog *San Francisco Schtuff*, May 6, 2003

CHAPTER 1

TOP OF THE HILL

One of the first buildings on Potrero Hill was probably this adobe on what is Twentieth Street today. This photograph was taken about 1900. An unknown early Potrero Hill historian wrote that it "was built by the Spaniards" and went on to describe its amenities: 4-foot-wide window sills, a sink and a water pump in the kitchen, and a fence built by a Mr. Thomson. Sarah Turnock is said to have moved there the year Lincoln died, and the "hills were full of beautiful wild flowers and on the old fences were very small owls." (Courtesy California Historical Society, FN-36142.)

At the far left of the *c.* 1900 photograph below is a glimpse of the old adobe house shown on the previous page. It was behind what is now 1929 Twentieth Street, between Carolina and De Haro Streets. The adobe was torn down in the early 1920s. It is rumored that remnants of it can still be unearthed in number 1929's backyard. The house on the right has been expanded and remodeled. (Then image, courtesy California Historical Society, FN-22184.)

Historians owe a great debt to San Francisco's Department of Public Works (DPW). In the early 1900s, the DPW began documenting its work on the streets, byways, and infrastructure of the city. A treasure trove of its photographs is available for viewing in the San Francisco History Center at the Main Library. Above, a DPW image shows a steam shovel grading Twentieth Street between De Haro and Carolina Streets in November 1915; the noise and the dirt fairly leap off the page. At the upper left of both of these images, a house or two down from the horizon, can be detected the Ramon-Hawes house on the southeast corner of Twentieth and Wisconsin Streets. (Then image, courtesy San Francisco History Center, San Francisco Public Library [SFPL].)

John Warnock was an Irish sailor who became a station engineer for PG&E (Pacific Gas and Electric) at Pennsylvania and Twenty-second Streets, where the Municipal Railway's Woods Yard is located today. His children, Irene and Robert, are shown above in front of the home he built at 1419 Twentieth Street in 1911. He later built two other houses on Twentieth Street—number 1415 in 1916 and number 1409 in 1917. The wood plank sidewalk is long gone, but otherwise 1419 is almost unchanged and is larger inside than its facade suggests. (Then image, courtesy Devito family.)

This San Francisco Stick–style house on the southeast corner of Twentieth and Wisconsin Streets was built *c.* 1885 by either dairyman Charles Hawes, who had a farmhouse and a large barn a block east, or by a Mr. Ramon, who is said to have been a descendant of Spanish settlers. This house, the farm buildings nearby, and the surrounding pastures were known as the Ramon-Hawes Ranch. Shortly after the 1981 photograph (below) was taken, a new owner replaced the siding with stucco, installed a swimming pool in the backyard, and planted the exotic vegetation that partially obscures the house from view today. It has a twin at 468 Mississippi Street. (Then image, photograph by Stephen Fotter.)

Businesses have come and gone along Twentieth Street between Arkansas and Connecticut Streets, but these two images prove that the overall look of this stretch of street has remained pretty much the same for more than 50 years. In 1951, Atchison's Pharmacy had a long soda fountain counter, and in later years, hill residents found the tiny post office substation located in the back convenient. Atchison's closed in 1995. All States Best Foods market occupies the building today, and across the street the Potrero Branch Library is undergoing major renovation.

A business that came to Twentieth Street in the 1950s and remains there still is Flo's Barber Shop. Florindo Cimino lives in the house he was born in on Potrero Hill. He attended Commerce High School and Modern Barber College at the same time, and he opened his shop at 1532 Twentieth Street in 1952. The image at left appeared on his first barber's license. Potrero Hill boasts one older family-owned business, Strand Service-Appliance, but Flo's, unlike Strand, has remained in one spot all these years. Many of Flo's customers have been his friends since childhood, and they call (415) 642-0887 for an appointment. His son Sal is also a barber. (Then image, courtesy Flo Cimino.)

Above is a 1924 view from Twentieth Street of Daniel Webster Elementary School under construction. The handsome brick building was torn down in the early 1970s and was replaced by something rather undistinguished. These adjunct portable classrooms were installed in the play yard and are visible along Twentieth Street today. In 2006, when many San Francisco schools were threatened with closure because of declining enrollment, Potrero Hill parents organized a successful campaign to "Save Daniel Webster." (Then image, courtesy SFPL.)

For more than 100 years, the water tank at Carolina and Twenty-second Streets was a neighborhood landmark. The original green wooden tank is shown here in a 1927 drawing by a student from the Rudolph Schaeffer School of Design on Mariposa Street. Pete Loskutoff remembers a Mr. Suder, the tank caretaker, whose perk for a number of years was a house on Twenty-second Street. In the 1950s, the wooden tank was replaced by a much larger, powder blue, metal tank. In 2006, that tank was demolished, but the reservoir, the city's fourth oldest, was retrofitted and remains.

The 1922 image looks northwest from Carolina Street at Twenty-second Street. The store at the corner of Twenty-second (far left) did a brisk business in polly (sunflower) seeds, a favorite snack of the Molokan community, and sold pickles from a big wooden barrel. In 1924, Southern Heights Avenue was cut through two blocks diagonally between Rhode Island and Carolina Streets— where a Twenty-first Street should have been— and is shown in the 2008 photograph as it curves into Carolina at the top of the hill.

A stucco apartment building, known at one time as the Sasoura house, for many years on Southern Heights Avenue between Carolina and De Haro Streets just east of the Neighborhood House. It played a cameo role in the 1981 movie *Chu Chu and the Philly Flash*, starring Carol Burnett. Later it burned, and its remains were a depressing sight until they were finally razed and replaced by another apartment building, looking vaguely Victorian and painted in pastel shades. Some of the best views of the city can be had from here. (Then image, photograph by Stephen Fotter.)

In 1907, Vic and Ermina Calegari built a house at Eighteenth and Arkansas Streets and opened the Bay View Grocery on the ground floor. Lorenzo Maggioncalda ran it after the Calegaris. Today Masoud Mostofi operates Chat's Coffee and Teas out of the same building. For several years, Chat's has provided desserts for the barbecue held each October on Potrero Hill History Night. (Then image, courtesy Calegari family.)

Bert Kloehn bought the Strand Service gas station on Third and Mariposa Streets in 1936, and began dispensing phonograph records and toasters as well as automotive services. When he decided to deal with appliances only, he relocated his business several times before buying the building at 344 Connecticut Street, formerly Ferrari's Hardware, in 1963. Shown below with Bert at the old gas station is his sister-in-law Sophie Sullivan. Today his daughter Judie Kloehn Lopez (left) is the resident proprietor of Strand Service—Appliances where Nipper, RCA Victor's "spokesdog," holds pride of place in the store's window. (Then image, courtesy Judie Kloehn Lopez.)

Artist Charles Griffin Farr moved to 733 De Haro Street in 1954. He painted *Potrero Hillside* (below), the view from his back deck, in 1965 and felt it was one of his most important works. Saint Teresa's Church is at top left; the old brick Daniel Webster School is at top center. Goats once roamed the empty block along Wisconsin Street; human kids played there too. Victoria Mews fills the site today. (Then image, courtesy Capricorn Gallery.)

Hill residents wondered what was coming when that "Potrero Hillside" block, bordered by Carolina, Wisconsin, Nineteenth, and Twentieth Streets, was cleared without warning in the 1970s. The Victoria Mews condominium complex opened there in 1978 with 84 condominiums, 10 offices, a swimming pool, a spa, and gardens. It was one of the first big condo projects in the city and the beginning of gentrification on Potrero Hill. The monthly dues, originally $84, are $500 today. (Then image, courtesy the *Potrero View*.)

The 200-seat Alta nickelodeon ("the Nick") opened in 1913 on Connecticut Street, a door or two up from Eighteenth Street. The little theater building still stands and has had a number of occupants over the years. It was renamed the New Potrero in 1929. The above image is from a 1932 home movie of a procession that started from St. Teresa's Church just a block away; to the right there is a glimpse of the famous creamery, where Goat Hill Pizza is located today. The photograph below, taken by Jo Babcock around 1979, shows the theater as the Lighthouse Church. (Then image, courtesy Berelich family.)

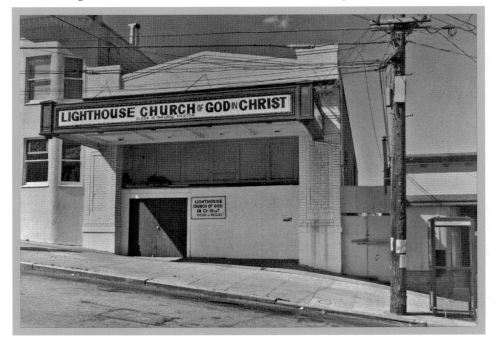

The image below was taken in 1968, when the defunct theater served briefly as a practice studio for the Grateful Dead. That is Jerry Garcia to right of the flower. Today the building is home to the Gurdjieff Society. The marquee is gone, but other aspects of the facade remain much the same. (Then image, courtesy Michael Ochs Archives/ Getty Images.)

Since 1990, many Hill residents have been celebrating Halloween by joining Farley's Pet Parade. It is made up mostly of dogs, but cats, parrots, and even goldfish and iguanas have participated in the march up Eighteenth Street to Texas Street, where Roger Hillyard, the proprietor of Farley's, awards trophies to virtually everyone. In recent years, a collie made a spot-on Mother Teresa, and this Chihuahua made a terrific bumblebee. Virginia Bertich, dressed for Halloween in 1924, would have enjoyed the fun and would have been welcome even without a pet. (Then image, courtesy Virginia Bertich Carlton.)

Virginia Bertich's older sister Bernice (left) and a friend pose a couple houses up the street from the Bertich home at 327 Missouri Street in 1920. David Bertich, Bernice and Virginia's father, was born to Italian parents but never spoke Italian because he was afraid it might give him an accent. He took the name of his Slovenian stepfather but shortened it from Berticevich to Bertich. The Bertich house is now owned by Mary Wasserman. Adan and Jaclyn Shaw, who live down the street, pose in front of it in the 2008 image. (Then image, courtesy Virginia Bertich Carlton.)

Between 1933 and 1958, John Sanguinetti's Fortuna Market was *the* place to shop at 1457 Eighteenth Street. In 1974, the Good Life Grocery took over that distinction and space and is shown here in 1979. Next door was a tiny Greek restaurant. Eighteenth Street has become a destination for foodies in recent years. Today Eliza's Restaurant occupies the site, and the Good Life flourishes on Twentieth Street. Eliza's neighboring eateries, watering holes, cafes, and snack shops include Chez Papa, Chez Maman, Baked, Lingba Lounge, Baraka, Aperto, Goat Hill Pizza, Hazel's, Farley's, Bloom's, and Chat's. Along Eighteenth Street, between Arkansas and Texas Streets, one cannot possibly go hungry—or thirsty—these days. (Then image, photograph by Stephen Fotter.)

Thirteen World War II–era public housing buildings once stood where a school stands today. (De Haro and Carolina Streets are mislabeled; both are one block east.) In the early 1960s, when the city announced plans to replace these buildings with even denser housing, Potrero Hill parents campaigned for a junior high school to be built instead. After many delays, Potrero Hill Junior High opened at 655 De Haro Street in 1972. Thomas Sammon was the first principal. The school later became the Potrero Hill Middle School, then Enola Maxwell Middle School of the Arts, and is now International Studies Academy, where "the knowledge, skills, and attitudes necessary to live in a global community" are promoted. (Then image, courtesy SFPL.)

Ten homes were moved or torn down by the city in 1951 to make room for an expansion and play yard at Patrick Henry School on Vermont Street. Babette Drefke is shown below with her infant daughter Wendy on the steps of her house at 634 Kansas Street shortly before it was moved up the hill. Drefke tried to make sure that the city would cover moving expenses. Her house was the last to go. Today she and Wendy Drefke Shinbori stand at the relocated house at 701 Kansas Street. (Then image, courtesy Babette Drefke.)

In 1919, the Presbyterian Women's Synodical Society of California Home Missions commissioned architect Julia Morgan (later famous for her work on Hearst Castle) to design a community center for the Russian immigrants who had fled Czarist oppression and settled on Potrero Hill shortly after the 1906 earthquake. The Potrero Hill Neighborhood House (called the Nabe by locals) opened in 1922 at 953 De Haro Street. In 1924, when Southern Heights Avenue was cut through, the building was moved 90 feet to the north but kept its original address. The Nabe was designated a historic landmark in 1976. Keith Goldstein, president of the Potrero Hill Association of Merchants and Businesses, is pictured in front of the Nabe in 2008. (Then image, courtesy Lew Baer.)

The big house anchoring the northwest corner of Eighteenth and Missouri Streets was built in 1905 and can be seen from many parts of the Hill. Christopher's Books has occupied the storefront since 1991. Previous tenants include Wulzen's Pharmacy (1930s and 1940s), the Little Red Door Thrift Shop (1970s), and Mary Price Flowers (1980s). In 1975, tie-dyed curtains hung in the window of the apartment that was home to the Free Angela Davis committee. Two movies, *Burglar* (1987) and *Sweet November* (2001), featured scenes shot in the upper apartment and in the streets and businesses nearby.

NORTH

Jackson Playground, bordered by Seventeenth, Arkansas, Mariposa, and Carolina Streets, has been a neighborhood gathering place since the early 1900s. In 1912, it was described as "the largest and most beautiful playground this side of Chicago, and second in the United States." Virginia Bertich is shown at the far right playing with friends there in 1918. The recreation center building was moved to the corner of Mariposa and Arkansas Streets around 1960. (Then image, courtesy Virginia Bertich Carlton.)

Pacific Rolling Mill opened on Potrero Point in 1866 and was the first significant steel mill in the West. It supplied structural steel, castings, and other materials to the builders of ships, mining equipment, and railroads. In 1900, Risdon Iron Works purchased the property, and the rolling mill, seen below about 1920, relocated to Seventeenth and Mississippi Streets. San Francisco Scrap Metals has been recycling nonferrous metal at this site since 1988. (Then image, courtesy Virginia Bertich Carlton.)

Salvotti's lunchroom on the corner of Seventeenth and Connecticut Streets looks pretty forlorn in the photograph above, which was taken shortly before owner Jules Salvotti sold it in 1975. Built by his parents, Guiseppe and Hilda Salvotti, with lumber salvaged from a post-1906-earthquake recovery shack, it opened as Hilda's Saloon in 1907. Back then, Mission Bay was less than a block away, and during the rainy season, the saloon was frequently flooded. Between 1975 and 1988, the restaurant changed hands a number of times and has been the Connecticut Yankee since 1989. (Then image, photograph by Stephen Fotter.)

Vermont Street at Sixteenth Street is shown above as it looked in 1929 when it was part of an industrial zone to the north of Potrero Hill. In the early 1900s, the Hill's northern shore on Mission Bay was several blocks east on Sixteenth Street. Today the 101 Freeway passes by to the left, Showplace Square decorator showrooms are nearby, and Station No. 29 of the San Francisco Fire Department is on the right. (Then image, courtesy SFPL.)

Looking north on Potrero Avenue onto Division Street in the 1940s, the Richwood Sanitary Building, 290 Division Street, was straight ahead. The building was later owned by Henry Calvin Fabrics and today is home to 10 businesses, including a training gym, a ski shop, architects, and Potrero Chiropractors and Acupuncture, while traffic on the 101 Freeway rumbles above. (Then image, courtesy private collector.)

Long Bridge once spanned Mission Bay, connecting downtown San Francisco to Potrero Hill. Kentucky Street (now Third Street) continued south. The *c.* 1900 photograph below looks north on Kentucky from Mariposa Street. Ships anchor at the Arctic Oil Works on the right. The neighborhood's first library is in the cluster of buildings at the left, and the eastern slopes of Potrero Hill are being chipped away for industrial expansion. Today tracks of Third Street Light Rail have replaced those of the Market Street Railway, and the Giants baseball park is in the distance. (Then image, courtesy Glenn Koch.)

Mission Creek originally meandered east from Mission Dolores through mudflats to the bay. The creek's use as a dump in the 1800s earned it the nickname "Shit Creek." In the late 1960s, houseboats from Islais Creek began moving into what had been an active shipping center along Mission Creek. In 1976, the houseboat owners and the San Francisco Port reached an agreement that insured the future of the houseboat community. Today Mission Creek Harbor, with 55 berths, is a diverse neighborhood of residents and boaters whose stewardship protects a unique San Francisco treasure in the midst of the city's newest neighborhood, Mission Bay. (Then image, photograph by Mel Orton.)

Third Street Bridge opened to great fanfare on May 12, 1933. It is a trunnion bascule bridge designed by Joseph Strauss, designer of the Golden Gate Bridge. A huge, elevated, concrete block serves as a counterweight to raise and lower its single span, allowing boats to pass between the bay and Mission Creek. The bridge, designated as San Francisco Landmark No. 194, is known today as Lefty O'Doul Bridge. The Giants baseball stadium (at this writing called AT&T Park) rises behind it—the only ballpark in America where home runs can be "splash hits." (Then image, courtesy SFPL; Now image, photograph by Stephen Fotter.)

The 1970s photograph looks across China Basin toward downtown and shows the buildings and mechanisms of the old Santa Fe Railroad train ferry slip. (A pier with a similar structure juts into the bay farther south, near Pier 54.) The Giants baseball park now stands on the northern shore of China Basin on land once called Steamboat Point, which was the site of a bustling hay dock in the 1890s. China Basin is now unofficially known as McCovey Cove in honor of Willie "Stretch" McCovey, the Giants great first baseman. Will Behrends's bronze statue of "Stretch" McCovey was unveiled in China Basin Park in 2003. (Both images, photographs by Stephen Fotter.)

The Mission Bay neighborhood's 325 acres are roughly bordered by Channel Street (aka Mission Creek), the San Francisco Bay, Mariposa Street, and Seventh Street. Originally Mission Bay was a body of water, which was gradually filled in from the 1860s through the early 1900s. It became a center for railroads and the shipping industry. These warehouses at Channel and Owens Streets (pictured below) are reminders of those days. Today a new community is taking shape. Condominium towers, parks, stores, restaurants, and the research campus of the University of California–San Francisco (UCSF) are rising there. The 2008 image is a view north across Koret Quad from UCSF's Genentech Hall.

CHAPTER

3

EAST

The discovery of gold in 1849 turned the tiny town of San Francisco into a bustling city and changed Point San Quentin (later known as Potrero Point and today as Pier 70) on Potrero Hill's San Francisco Bay shoreline into a hub of industry. This *c.* 1900 photograph looks northwest from around Illinois and Twentieth Streets toward St. Teresa's Church at its original Nineteenth and Tennessee Streets location. The horses shown here hauled equipment around the yards of Union Iron Works and Pacific Rolling Mill. Many of Potrero Point's workers, including Irish, Scotch, Dutch, Italian, and Russian immigrants, lived nearby on Scotch Hill, Irish Hill (demolished during World War I), or in Dutchman's Flat, today known as Dogpatch. (Courtesy California Historical Society, FN-36547.)

HOOPER LUMBER CO.

In the late 1800s, the Hooper Lumber Company stood on landfill at Seventeenth and Illinois Streets on Central Basin. More of the basin was filled in, and by 1940, when this wooden building with its rounded roof was built at 555 Illinois Street, the shoreline was a block farther east. C. F. Hendry Company, a venerable ship chandlery, occupied the building in the late 1940s and early 1950s. Known today as the Bluepeter building, after a design firm that was a tenant for many years, it is one of the few buildings remaining in the Mission Bay area that connect the neighborhood to its rich maritime history.

Bert Kloehn bought the Strand Service gas station on Third Street at Mariposa Street from Larry Strand in 1936. Kloehn sold records there as well, and he met Frank Sinatra through this unusual sideline. Today a condominium project fills the lot. During the dot-com boom of the 1990s, live-work lofts like these sprouted all over the Hill. Intended for artists and craftspeople, market rates pushed the units far beyond their reach, inspiring the nickname "lawyer-lofts." (Then image, courtesy Judie Kloehn Lopez.)

Between 1903 and 1907, several bridges were constructed between Pennsylvania Avenue and Minnesota Street. They spanned the sheer escarpment that resulted when chunks of the hill were removed during the laying of railroad tracks. Until 1924, Saint Teresa's Church stood a block from the foot of the Nineteenth Street pedestrians-only bridge, seen below. Anne Loskutoff, wearing a suit, gloves, and high heels, remembered going "clippety-clip" over the Twentieth Street span to get to her job at the American Can Company in the 1940s. (Then image, courtesy Saint Teresa's Church.)

Saint Teresa's Church, seen at left *c.* 1915, was built in 1892 on the northeast corner of Nineteenth (then called Butte) and Tennessee Streets. By 1924, the area had become increasingly industrial, and more and more parishioners found homes higher on the hill. The church followed them. It was cut in half and hauled up the hill to its present location on Nineteenth and Connecticut Streets. Soon after the move, the bell tower was remodeled, and the building was stuccoed. (Then image, courtesy Saint Teresa's Church.)

Major chapters of U.S. history can be read through the industries that grew and flourished on Potrero Hill's waterfront, seen here from Nineteenth Street and Pennsylvania Avenue in the 1930s. Union Iron Works (UIW) manufactured locomotives, mining equipment of every description, and ships for the Spanish-American War. After being bought by Bethlehem Steel in 1905, it built ships for both

world wars. In the 2008 image, the I-280 Freeway dominates the foreground, gantry cranes hover just east of Illinois Street at Nineteenth Street, ships being repaired at San Francisco drydock can be seen in the distance, and the Mission Bay campus of UCSF rises to the north. Most of the historic shipyard buildings of UIW/Bethlehem are vacant at the moment, awaiting creative reuse.

During the two world wars, Bethlehem Shipbuilding Corporation constructed 156 ships, 20 submarines, and repaired more than 3,000 vessels at Potrero Point/Pier 70. Below, a crowd of 15,000 workers jams Twentieth Street east of Illinois Street in the 1940s as Vice Adm. John Wills Greenslade presents a job-well-done award to general manager A. S. Gunn. The shipyard's administration building, erected in 1917, is seen at the right in both images. (Then image, courtesy private collector.)

Peoples Cafe, shops, and a bank occupied the west side of Third Street between Twentieth and Nineteenth Streets in 1920. St. Teresa's Church on Tennessee Street can be seen behind them. All served the workers in industries along Potrero Hill's waterfront. Until recently, Pro Camera occupied the corner of Twentieth and Third Streets in a building that once housed the Anglo California National Bank. (Then image, courtesy Bancroft Library, University of California–Berkeley.)

American Can Company opened a new factory between Third, Illinois, Twentieth, and Twenty-second Streets in 1916. It was the largest manufacturer of tin cans in the United States and the last big industry to construct a major facility in the Potrero Point/Pier 70 industrial zone. At one time, it was the single largest employer of Dogpatch residents. The plant closed in 1969. It is now the American Industrial Center and houses some 300 commercial tenants, including many artists, nonprofits, and the *Potrero View*, the neighborhood's monthly newspaper. The newsboys in the 1920s image above are perhaps waiting for workers to stream out of American Can at closing time. (Then image, courtesy California Historical Society, FN-36596.)

Around 1870, Market Street Railway built a carbarn on Kentucky Street near Twenty-third Street. It was nicknamed "My Old Kentucky Home." Below, on May 10, 1941, Car No. 871 of the 22 Fillmore line pulls out for the last time. New coaches replaced the 22 line of streetcars, and the barn was torn down. The 2008 image above shows the tracks of the Third Street Light Rail, which opened on January 13, 2007, linking downtown to the city's underserved southeastern neighborhoods. On Illinois Street between Twenty-fifth and Twenty-sixth Streets is the huge new light rail maintenance facility built by the Municipal Railway (Muni). (Then image, courtesy SFPL.)

The photograph below appeared in the *Daily Herald* in 1921: "The tall building on the left is the Potrero Hotel, where federal drys uncovered lively liquor caches and sales places. Building on extreme right is Potrero Police Station. Close quarters for bootleggers you might say." Between the station, built in 1912, and the hotel was Community Hospital. The station has been empty since 1993, when police operations moved to the Bayview district. (Then image, courtesy SFPL.)

Noted photographer Minor White (1908–1976) took this image looking east from Iowa Street near Twenty-second Street in 1949. The massive gas tanks no longer exist, nor does White's hillside vantage point, which was displaced by the I-280 Freeway. But the warehouse on the left remains and is today the set-building workshop of the San Francisco Opera. Three of the houses on Minnesota Street also survive. (Then image, courtesy California Historical Society, FN-03045; copyright by the Trustees of Princeton University.)

The Potrero School was built on Minnesota Street near Twenty-second Street in 1877. As the population of Dogpatch grew, an addition was needed. The new building, constructed in 1895 on the same lot but on Tennessee Street, was named for its benefactor, Irving M. (I. M.) Scott, the dynamic superintendent of Union Iron Works. The first building, shown above in the early 1900s (the addition just visible behind it), was eventually torn down. The 2008 image, taken on Minnesota Street, shows the back of I. M. Scott and a play yard where the original school stood. It is the city's oldest school building and was declared a San Francisco Historic Landmark in 1985. (Then image, courtesy SFPL.)

Minor White took a number of photographs in the Dogpatch neighborhood between 1946 and 1953 when, together with Ansel Adams, he taught photography at the California School of Fine Arts. This building in the 1100 block Tennessee Street intrigued him, as did several similar ones in the same area. All are gone now, which is a pity because no examples of this style remain on the hill today. The modern building shown in the 2008 image above stands on the approximate site and vaguely reflects its predecessor. (Then image, courtesy California Historical Society, FN-03052; copyright by the Trustees of Princeton University.)

Between 1904 and 1907, Southern Pacific Railroad tore out most of Potrero Hill's eastern slope during construction of an improved route to San Jose called the Bayshore Cutoff. The new route included five tunnels. The 1905 image below looks south from about Iowa and Twenty-second Streets, and shows excavation (at center) for the double-bore Tunnel No. 2. The hillside at right was known as Poppy Hill by locals. The 2008 image above, taken from the 280 Freeway, shows a glimpse of the tunnel opening at far left and the San Francisco Food Bank on Pennsylvania Avenue. (Then image, courtesy California Historical Society, FN-36613.)

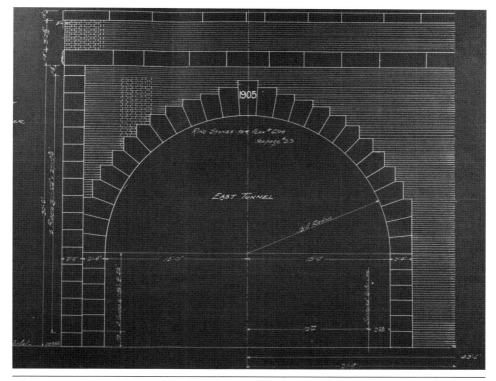

Shown above is a blueprint of Southern Pacific's Tunnel No. 1, which runs between Mariposa and Twenty-second Streets. In a special edition of the *Call* published in 1912, a young I. M. Scott student wrote, "The three important railroads run through the Potrero, or rather, under it." The 2008 shot looks north through the tunnel from the Caltrain station at Twenty-second Street and Pennsylvania Avenue.

Several huge gas tanks once stood on Potrero Hill. This 1976 painting by John Almond, which hangs in the lobby of San Francisco General Hospital, shows one of them looming over a small Victorian house on Pennsylvania Avenue at Twenty-third Street. The Victorian still stands. Where the tank once stood is now occupied by the San Francisco Food Bank, located at 900 Pennsylvania Street, which collects food from growers, grocers, and manufacturers and distributes it to almost 500 local agencies.

CHAPTER 4

SOUTH

Islais Creek is the natural southern boundary of Potrero Hill. Here is the Islais Bridge on Third Street under construction in 1949. In the 1950s, the creek was the center of the world's largest sardine canning industry. Today most of the creek's watershed is filled in, but some headwaters still flow in Glen Canyon Park 3 miles to the west. (Courtesy private collector.)

The Quonset hut—style Potrero Hill Recreation Center has been a familiar sight at the top of the hill's southeastern slope since the 1950s. Jon Greenberg was its director from 1966 until 2008. The center has a gymnasium, a sports field, basketball and tennis courts, a playground, a picnic area, amazing views, and a mural featuring football's O. J. Simpson, who grew up on the hill. A lone Victorian stood on the site in the 1940s. The Bay Bridge and the top floor of Daniel Webster School are seen in the distance in the image below. (Then image, courtesy private collector.)

These two images look northeast along De Haro Street from Twenty-fifth Street. The 1941 photograph above shows De Haro before it was paved. Today planting has replaced the rubble of the median strip, adding lushness to this still-rustic stretch of De Haro Street.

A steam shovel was grading Rhode Island Street just south of Twenty-second Street on April 12, 1916, preparing it for paving. The small market at center was typical of those found on almost every block of Potrero Hill. If customers called before a certain hour, their groceries would be delivered to their door.

Below, standing in front of their grandparents' house at 1029 Carolina Street in 1943 are, from left to right, Jack Bogdanoff, Patricia Bataiff, Allen Raymond, Elsie Whitlow, and Rich Forslund. The grandparents, Joseph and Elsie Bataiff, came from Russia and attended the Molokan church two blocks north. Employees of the Potrero Hill Health Center, located just around the corner on Wisconsin Street, stand in the same spot in the 2008 image above. They are, from left to right, Corinna Neustaetter, director Sushma Magnuson, Anne Martinez, LaRhonda Reddic, Mary G. Pastor, and Leonard Williams. (Then image, courtesy Bataiff, Passarelli, and Whitlow families.)

The 1929 photograph below looks south on Carolina Street from a vantage point just up the street from where the photographs on the previous page were taken. The house with the peaked roof on its porch at the far left is 1015 Carolina Street and appears in both these images. The median strip between Twenty-second and Twenty-third Streets was constructed in 1931. Residents have done most of the planting. South of Twenty-third Street is Starr King Open Space. (Then image, courtesy SFPL.)

The public housing built along Carolina Street south of Twenty-third Street during World War II was torn down in the 1960s, but remains of the foundations littered the landscape well into the 1970s. After the land was sold to a private developer, a group of Potrero Hill activists formed a land trust, out of which was born Starr King Open Space. The unfenced, 3.5-acre parcel's native species and serpentine soil are reminders of what Potrero Hill was like 100 years ago. In the background at left is Starr King Elementary School. In 2006, the school started a Mandarin immersion program for children of all backgrounds that has been extremely successful. (Then image, courtesy the *Potrero View*.)

The trestle spanning Army Street at Mississippi Street was built in the early 1900s during Southern Pacific Railroad's construction of the Bayshore Cutoff, one of the most expensive sections of the cutoff. The 1917 image of it (above) looks east. Before 1891, Army was Colusa Street; it was one of more than a dozen streets in the Potrero area named for California counties around the time California was admitted to the United States in 1850. In 1995, Army was renamed Cesar Chavez Street to honor the founder of the United Farm Workers. (Then image, courtesy SFPL.)

SOUTH

The 1928 image above looks east on Army Street from Connecticut Street and shows the former freight-only track of the Ocean Shore Railway. Called the "Industrial Lead," it ran along Army from Evans Avenue to Illinois Street and provided interchange with both the Western Pacific and Santa Fe Railroads. After the 1906 earthquake, Ocean Shore was awarded $15,000 to fill in the "Precita Valley Swamp," bordered by Potrero Avenue, Army Street, Alabama Street, and Serpentine Avenue, which it did using rubble from the quake. (Then image, courtesy SFPL.)

The Islais Incinerator Plant is shown under construction in the 1920 photograph (below), which looks southwest from Army Street at Kansas Street. The shops of the Ocean Shore Railroad are clustered on the flats below Bernal Heights. The railroad was intended to link San Francisco and Santa Cruz. Construction started in 1905 but was delayed by the 1906 earthquake and was never completed. This section of track was taken over by Western Pacific and was used until the mid-1980s. The 101/James Lick Freeway spans the site today. (Then image, courtesy SFPL.)

Between the attack on Pearl Harbor in December 1941 and the end of World War II in August 1945, industry boomed in the Potrero, and the workforce more than doubled. Housing was built for the influx of wartime workers and their families on the south slopes of the hill and along the Army Street corridor. Victorian-style homes and sleek condos have replaced some of the wartime housing. Residents of the remaining public housing fear that future developments could force them out. Today the 101 Freeway spans Army Street, which is now called Cesar Chavez Street.

The 1928 photograph above looks south from Marin Street at sewer pipes being laid along Third Street. The hills of the Bayview district can be seen in the background. Today two passenger platforms for the Third Street Light Rail are at the same location.

CHAPTER 5

WEST

In 1854, eight members of the Catholic religious order Sisters of Mercy sailed from Ireland, bound for San Francisco. Led by Sister Mary Baptist Russell, age 25, the group arrived three months later. They immediately set to work caring for the sick, the indigent, and the exploited, and they opened St. Mary's Hospital on Stockton Street in 1857. In 1869, the Magdalen Asylum, a home for wayward girls, was built on Potrero Avenue and Twenty-first Street. It was renamed St. Catherine's Home and Training School in 1904. Today all that remains of St. Catherine's is the Lourdes Grotto alongside San Francisco General Hospital's Mental Health and Rehabilitation Center. A Healing Garden, designed by Potrero Hill's Topher Delaney, is nearby. (Courtesy the Bancroft Library, University of California–Berkeley.)

San Francisco General Hospital opened at 1001 Potrero Avenue in 1872. In 1915, buildings in a neo-Italian Renaissance style with patterned redbrick exteriors, terracotta, and marble trim and ornamentation were added. They are seen here in 1922. More buildings have risen on the hospital campus in the years since. The hospital is the only trauma center in the city and county of San Francisco. In 2008, an $800 million bond passed, proposing rebuilding to meet state seismic requirements. (Then image, courtesy SFPL; Now image, photograph by Stephen Fotter.)

The Cathedral Mission of the Good Samaritan was founded in the late 1890s by the Episcopal diocese to help new immigrants access needed services, develop self-sufficiency, and participate fully as members of the San Francisco community. Shortly after the 1906 earthquake, the Good Samaritans built a brown-shingled settlement house (pictured above) on Potrero Avenue at Twenty-fifth Street. The building was seriously damaged in the 1989 earthquake and was replaced in 1997 by the new Good Samaritan Family Resource Center, which includes 20 affordable family housing units. (Then image, courtesy private collector; Now image, photograph by Stephen Fotter.)

Both these photographs look north along Potrero Avenue toward San Francisco General Hospital from a vantage point on Bernal Heights, just south of Army/Cesar Chavez Street. James Lick Freeway and its profusion of ramps and overpasses dominate the 2008 image. Rolph Playground is on the left, and across the avenue is Potrero de Sol Park, which now includes a state-of-the-art skateboarding bowl. The old Good Samaritan Center can be seen at the upper left in the 1949 image.

Seals Stadium opened at Sixteenth and Bryant Streets in 1931. Built for the Seals and Mission Reds baseball teams of the Pacific Coast League, it was home to the National League Giants for two seasons following the team's move from New York in 1958 and was torn down after the 1959 season. The Giants began playing at the newly built Candlestick Park the next year. The Potrero Center opened on the site in 1996. Both photographs were taken from what was once the Seals Stadium office on the southeast corner of Potrero Avenue and Sixteenth Street. (Then image, courtesy SFPL.)

The California School of Mechanical Arts (CSMA), which occupied several buildings on the block bounded by Utah, San Bruno, Fifteenth, and Sixteenth Streets, is seen here from San Bruno and Sixteenth Streets around 1895, the year of its founding. The school offered free education to boys and girls, combining general academic preparation with technical and vocational training. The goal was to produce "the Educated Craftsman." CSMA would expand south to the block where UPS is today. The original site is now occupied by Bonham's and Butterfield's auction house.

Above, apprentices at the California School of Mechanical Arts (CSMA) put down an artificial stone floor near one of the school's shop buildings in the late 1890s. That floor has disappeared, but a fragment of an early CSMA building can be seen today in the parking lot of Bonham's along Utah Street. The school later became Lick-Wilmerding High School, and in 1955 it relocated to Ocean Avenue. The school's goal remains "to develop qualities of the head, heart, and hands."

A bequest from ranching heiress Miranda Lux established the Lux School of Industrial Training, which was dedicated to teaching girls to "do the common thing uncommonly well." The school occupied this building at 2450 Seventeenth Street at Potrero Avenue from 1913 until 1953, sharing an administration with nearby Lick-Wilmerding High School. The building had a rooftop playground, a recitation room, and a cooking laboratory. In 1990, it was bought by Soka Gakkai International (SGI), an American Buddhist organization that promotes world and individual happiness. Chanting *nam-myhoho-renge-kyo* is the primary practice of SGI's diverse membership. (Then image, copyright by Moulin Studios.)

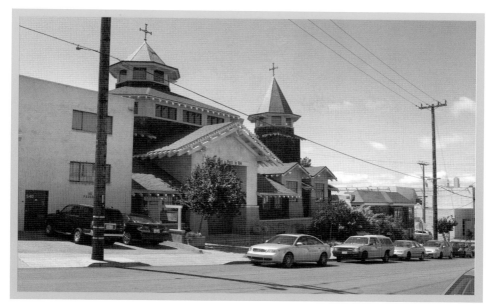

It is fitting that a Russian Orthodox priest once stored supplies for a program to feed the homeless in one of these buildings on De Haro Street between Mariposa and Eighteenth Streets. St. Gregory's of Nyssa Episcopal Church, which opened at 500 De Haro Street in 1995, carries on the benevolence to this day by offering free foodstuffs every Friday. Designer John Goldman won the American Institute of Architects Religious Architecture Award for this building. Artist Mark Dukes's mural *The Dancing Saints* encircles the church's rotunda. St. Gregory's is an intentional community whose members create the liturgy, the programs, and the activities of the church together. (Then image, courtesy St. Gregory's Church.)

The West Coast Recycling Company occupied a steel-covered warehouse at Rhode Island and Sixteenth Streets for many years. Towers of baled cardboard filled its cavernous interior. In 2004, the California Culinary Academy moved into a new building on the site, which includes Carême 350, a student-staffed restaurant. And there is a Starbucks on the corner.

In the early years of the 20th century, an industrial lumber-planing mill operated on the block bounded by Seventeenth, Rhode Island, Mariposa, and Kansas Streets. In the 1920s, automobile maintenance and repair shops moved in. S&C Ford occupied the site for many years and is shown above in 2001, just before its huge garage was torn down. The lot was a big hole for several years, inspiring locals to flights of fancy as to its possible reuse. They did not imagine that the so-called "Goat Hole" would become the site of a luxury condominium development called the Potrero with a Whole Foods grocery on the corner. (Then image, photograph by Stephen Fotter.)

These two photographs look down Twenty-fourth Street from De Haro Street toward the Mission District and Twin Peaks. In 1945, Jack O'Keefe's bar was at Twenty-fourth and Rhode Island Streets, and one block west stood the Dutch Boy Paint Factory on Kansas Street. In those pre-freeway days, Twenty-fourth Street went straight through, allowing residents easy access to the Mission District's many shops, restaurants, and movie theaters. Twenty-fourth Street between De Haro and Rhode Island Streets is still paved with bricks. (Then image, courtesy SFPL.)

Below is a closer view of the old paint factory taken in 1927, looking north on Kansas Street at Twenty-fourth Street. Paint was manufactured on this site from 1858 until 1970, when National Lead Company sold the property to Synanon, the controversial drug-rehabilitation organization. In 1979, a developer purchased the property but soon went bankrupt. In the late 1980s, after a thorough toxic cleanup, a more successful developer built the apartment and condominium complex that occupies the entire block today. The trees at left hide the 101/James Lick Freeway. (Then image, courtesy SFPL.)

Taken in the 1930s, the photograph below looks north on Vermont Street from Eighteenth Street. All the houses on the left were torn down or moved in the early 1950s to make way for the 101/ James Lick Freeway. The pointed roof at right is on 471 Vermont. Vangel and Vasila Theodos, natives of Albania, bought the house next door for $2,850 in 1920. The family sold it in 1991 for $295,000. The mind reels to contemplate what the house would fetch today. (Then image, courtesy Alcus Jefferson Jr.)

Potrero Hill's twisty Vermont Street is seen looking north from Twenty-second Street in the 1940s photograph above. Today trees obscure all seven curves (five full and two halves), but the house with a peaked turret (901 Vermont Street) can be seen in both images. McKinley Square at the top at Twentieth Street has a new children's playground, is a favorite place for dog walkers, and has panoramic views over the Mission District. (Then image, courtesy SFPL.)

Both images look south toward Nineteenth Street, where it dead ends, a block west of San Bruno Avenue. In the 1928 image, Utah Street is at the lower left. A curve of the 101/James Lick Freeway, built in the 1950s, obliterated Utah Street between Eighteenth and Twentieth Streets, and the 2008 image shows a private driveway where Utah once was. As to the curve, it is known as Hospital Curve either because of its proximity to San Francisco General Hospital or because the traffic accidents that happen along it often sent people there. (Then image, courtesy SFPL.)

WEST

Estelle West was once known as the "Goat Lady of Potrero Hill." She had a herd of 18 goats when her property between Utah Street and Potrero Avenue, just south of Nineteenth Street, was needed for the construction of the 101 Freeway. She put up a good fight, but she is pictured below in 1951, standing with several of her goats, amidst the ruins of her house. She sold her goats—$30 for the milk goats, $25 for the mom, and $12.50 to $15 for the others. A row of Victorians along Potrero Avenue is visible in the background of both images. (Then image, courtesy SFPL.)

These two photographs look north along the 101/ James Lick Freeway from Twenty-third Street toward the Twenty-second Street pedestrian bridge. The *c.* 1958 image below of the newly completed freeway shows just a few trees standing on the west slope of McKinley Square at Vermont and Twentieth Streets. (Then image, courtesy Tom Gray.)

Nick Radovich (center, in vest) stands in front of his saloon on Eighteenth Street at Vermont Street in 1906. His daughters Anna and Bella are at the far left. Nick paid for the transatlantic passage of his fellow Slovenian John Kambic (far right), who later became a builder and mover of houses. In 1927, the Slovenian community bought a building at 2101 Mariposa Street and named it Slovenian Hall. The Grape Festival and Blood Sausage Dinner and Dance held there still draw large crowds. In the 2008 image, at the site of the saloon, John Kreiden of Safety Training Seminars stands in front of his company's office. (Then image, courtesy Don Kambic.)

The image above looks north on Rhode Island Street from Twentieth Street around 1920. Directly ahead is the tall smokestack of a garbage incinerator near Seventh and Brannan Streets, known locally as the Crematory, or the Crim. Shura Fadeff remembers neighborhood kids salvaging "anything that you could find to use for something else," including parts for homemade, engine-less "cars" for the soapbox derbies down Carolina Street. There were several soap manufacturers on the fringes of Potrero Hill at the time, and actual soapboxes were plentiful for scrounging. (Then image, courtesy Bancroft Library, University of California–Berkeley.)

Jim Schetinin, Jackie Schetinin, and Shirley Durakoff lined up according to height against a utility pole in 1939. Behind them is William Schetinin's grocery at 1016 De Haro Street. The Schetinins were Russian Molokans, so the store did not sell pork products or alcohol. The Molokan community was once so large that the western side of Potrero Hill was known as Russian Hill, a sometimes confusing situation since there was, and is, another Russian Hill in a different part of town. The neighborhood called Potrero Hill is not a single hill or even entirely a hill—its ups and downs have been known by several names over the years. Those who live there just call it "The Hill." (Then image, courtesy Booth-Fisher family.)

ACROSS AMERICA, PEOPLE ARE DISCOVERING
SOMETHING WONDERFUL. *THEIR HERITAGE.*

Arcadia Publishing is the leading local history publisher in the United States. With more than 3,000 titles in print and hundreds of new titles released every year, Arcadia has extensive specialized experience chronicling the history of communities and celebrating America's hidden stories, bringing to life the people, places, and events from the past. To discover the history of other communities across the nation, please visit:

www.arcadiapublishing.com

Customized search tools allow you to find regional history books about the town where you grew up, the cities where your friends and family live, the town where your parents met, or even that retirement spot you've been dreaming about.

MAP SEARCH